A Kalmus Classic Edition

Louis
KÖHLER

THE LITTLE PIANIST

Opus 189

Arranged by E. BOSQUET

FOR SOLO PIANO

K 02209

C. L. H. KÖHLER

Chrétien Louis Henri Köhler, né à Brunswick en 1820 et mort à Königsberg en 1886, fut chef d'orchestre à Marienbourg, Elbing et Königsberg. Dans cette dernière ville, il dirigea encore la « Société des Chanteurs » et y fonda une école de piano et de théorie. Il fit aussi de la critique musicale.

C'était un éminent musicien, très versé en son art. Ses compositions, 3 opéras, 1 ballet, des chœurs et de nombreuses pièces pour le piano, ont du mérite. Köhler est surtout connu par ses écrits théoriques. Ses exercices pour le développement de la technique pianistique, dans le genre de ceux de Czerny, tendent aujourd'hui à reprendre une place importante dans l'enseignement. Ce sont des recueils soigneusement rédigés et gradués, constituant une excellente diversion aux ouvrages similaires de Czerny, dont ils diffèrent par leur caractère plus sévère.

Christian Ludwig Heinrich Köhler, der in Braunschweig im Jahre 1820 geboren wurde, 1886 in Königsberg starb, war Orchesterdirigent in Marienburg, Elbing und Königsberg. In der letzteren leitete er noch den Sängerverein und gründete eine Schule für Klavier und Theorie. Er war auch Musikkritiker.

Er war ein hervorragender Musiker, der seine Kunst beherrschte. Seine Kompositionen : 3 Opern, 1 Ballett, Chöre und zahlreiche Stücke für Klavier, sind beachtenswert. Köhler ist besonders durch seine theoretischen Schriften bekannt. Seine Uebungen zur Entwicklung der Klaviertechnik, in der Art von Czerny, wollen sich heute eine wichtige Stellung im Unterricht zurückerobern. Es sind sehr sorgfältig redigierte und progressiv angeordnete Sammlungen, die eine vorzügliche Abweichung von den ähnlichen Werken Czernys darstellen, von denen sie sich durch ihren strengeren Charakter unterscheiden.

Christian Louis Henry Köhler was born at Brunswick in 1820 and died at Königsberg in 1886. He was conductor of the orchestra at Marienburg, Elbing and Königsberg. In the latter town he also conducted the « Society of Singers » and founded a school for the piano and for theory. He was also musical critic.

He was an excellent musician well versed in his art. His compositions : 3 operas, 1 ballet, 2 choral works and many pieces for the piano, have some merit. Köhler is mostly known for his theoretical work. To-day there is a tendancy to give a considerable position in teaching to his exercises for the development of piano technique, which are in the style of those by Czerny. They represent a carefully revised and graduated collection forming an excellent diversion from similar works by Czerny, their character being more severe.

LE PETIT PIANISTE

The Little Pianist   -   Der Kleine Klavierspieler

LOUIS KÖHLER, Op. 189

4

9.
10.
11.

12.

13.

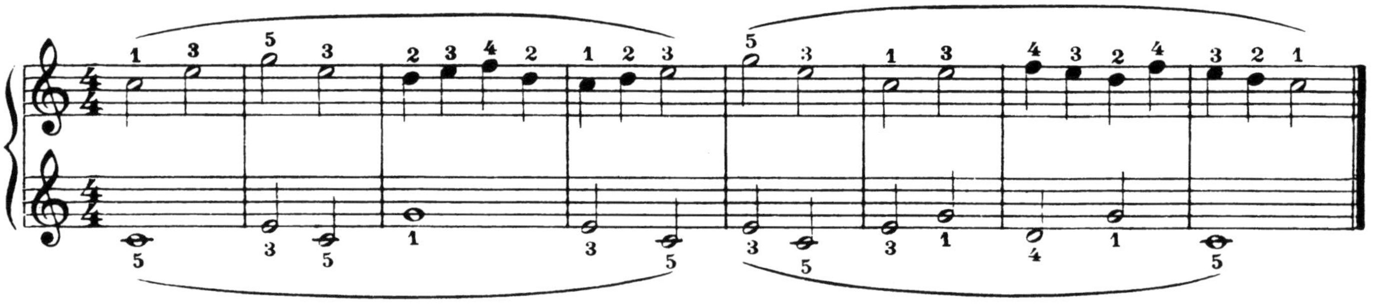

14.

15.

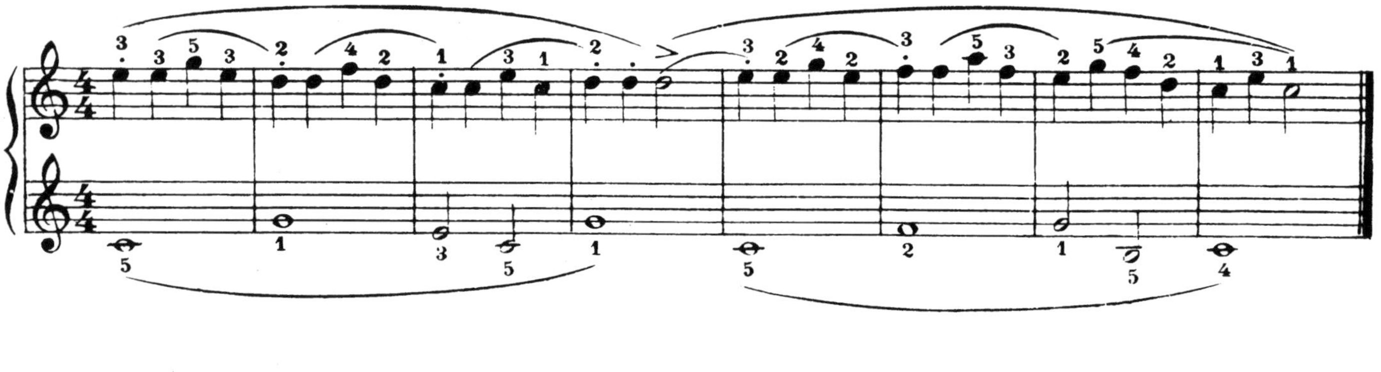

16.
17.
Fine
D.C. al Fine

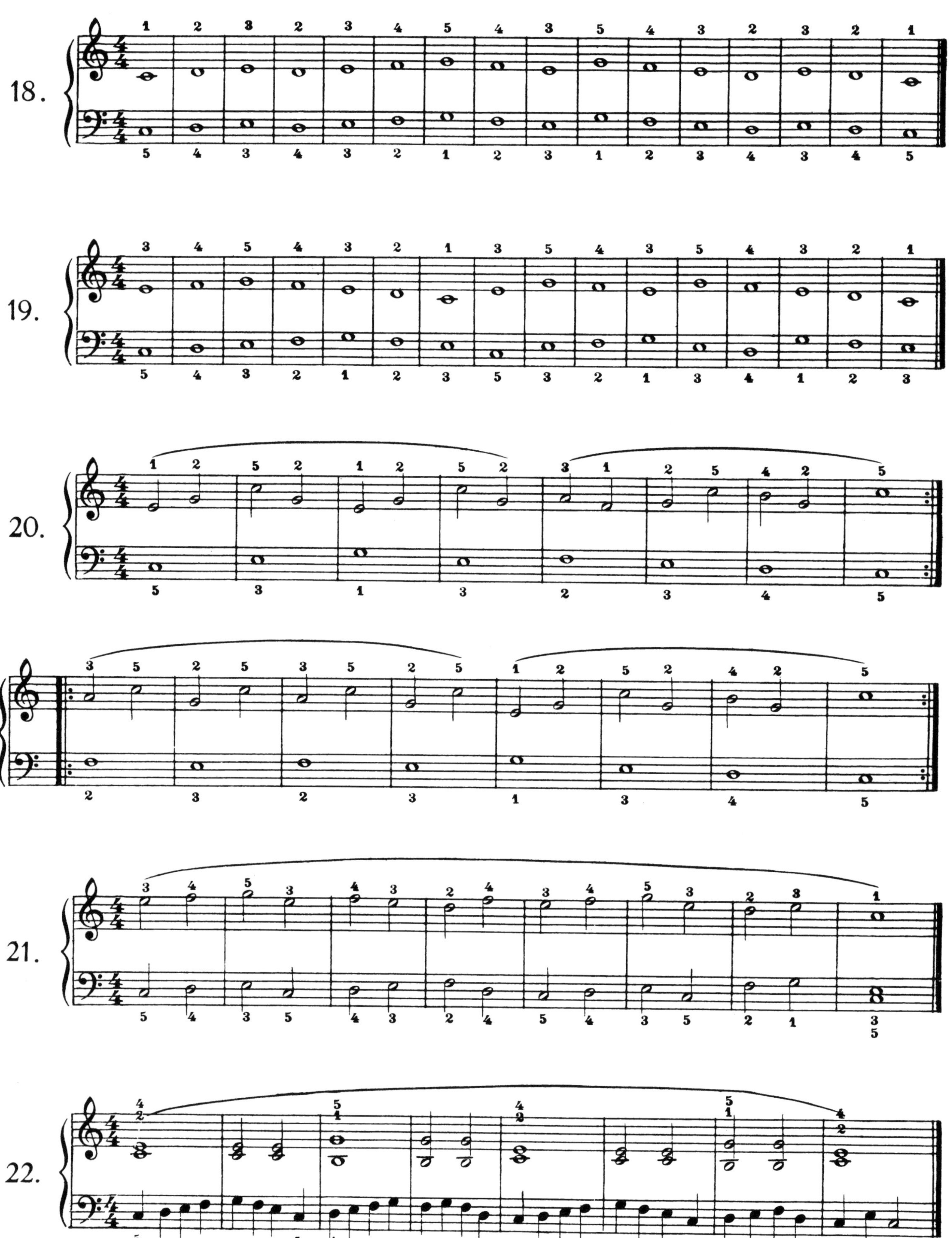

23.

24.

25.
Fine
D.C. al Fine
26.

27.

28.
29.
Fine

30.
D.C. al Fine

31.
32.

33.
Fine
D.C. al Fine
34.
Fine
D.C. al Fine

35.

36.
Fine
D.C. al Fine
37.

38.
Fine
39.
Fine
D.C. al Fine
1.
2.
D.C. al Fine.

40.